Beautifu

Catherine Bennett

BookLeaf
Publishing

India | USA | UK

Presentation by *BookLeaf Publishing*

Web: www.bookleafpub.com

E-mail: info@bookleafpub.com

ISBN: 9789358314274

First edition 2023

Hurt

Shall I compare you to a winter's night?
An icy frost ensnaring nature's life.
Your commands pierce like an east-wind's bite
Wounding hurtfully: cruel, dangerous knife.
I am lost and caught in this spiteful storm:
Savage hurt, blasting brain numb; gnarled-raw
I plead for the morn; weather to transform.
Melting, dissipating, gone: hard-hate thaw.
The ethereal moon guides me my door.
My protective angel, blanketing fears.
Conquering force, ice-warrior of war.
Defeating hurt; defending wasteful tears.
As long as hope strives warmth into my heart,
Hope shields hatred and makes demons depart.

Rejuvenation

I wear your love like a soft, woollen hat
Battling against the bitter, biting storm.
I lean upon your shirted shoulder that
Keeps me upright; you shape my form. Not torn.

I wear your hope like an invitation
Promoting a sense of optimism.
You are my friend; my rejuvenation.
Reflecting light. Illumination. Prism.

I wear your faith like a full, constant moon
Orbiting. Circling. My incessant force.
You are my song; my sweet, melodic tune.
Your words of strength, I listen and endorse.

Until eternity, my love is true.
Like the sun; radiating warmth and hue.

Imperfect Day

It is a hot, sunny day in July:
Birds are singing;
She is breathing.

The postman delivers her mail:
He is whistling;
She is breathing.

Outside in the yard, neighbours quietly hang out
their washing.
Inside, she slowly sips her tea;
She is breathing.

Nobody hears her inner torment; nobody hears
her silent cries.
The telephone rings.
She is breathing.

The decision is final.
She surrenders to the battle
She has fought so hard, for so long.

She finishes her tea.
Glances out of the window for the very, last
time.

Birds are singing.

But she no longer hears.

School Satchel Days

Life will never be the same again,
For the little boy who is nearly five.
He smells so crisp.
Neatly ironed. Brilliant, white shirt.
Brand new, grey shorts and stripy tie.
Showing off his 'Just William' knees.
Tight, laced-up shiny shoes – no scuffs allowed.

He asks: "Why do I have to wear these silly
clothes?"
The truth is softened by her buffering reply:
"So you look smart and respectable."
She does not disillusion him with the terrible
truth:
"Your life will never be the same again,
That tie is your leash, your noose, branding you
a position in society -
It symbolises restricting rules and eternal, tight
conformity."

The Birthday Picnic

The preparation seems endless:
A day of toy shops;
Buying food;
A day of buying things, previously forgotten.

The preparation seems endless:
Wrapping presents;
Blowing up balloons;
Making jellies.

When will the 'day before' ever end.
All of this, just for one day.
But what a special day, for such a special child.
Nobody is invited; apart from my family of five.

When school ends, we drive to a deserted,
idyllic spot.
A wide, open space with trees scattered around.
The sun's gentle rays force through the cotton
wool clouds.
The scene is beautiful. Magical.

The children run ahead: they are happy –
And so am I.

Phoenix Rising

Rising from the dark like a glorious red-dawn
sun
Blazing radiantly down upon the precious, azure
world.
Victorious day-star: emitting rays of hope,
recovery and renewal.

Rising from the mountain top like a soaring,
majestic bird
Spreading powerfully its glorious span; immense
and wise.
Elegant eagle: sublime visionary of insight and
guidance.

Rising from a deep sleep like an invigorated,
refreshed child
Emerging energized with a playful and pure
mind.
Innocent being: a beacon of light and
inspirational joy.

Rising from the meadow like a colourful, hot-air
balloon
Cradling eagerly its passengers; driving elation
and fear.

Happy adventurer: a provider of undiscovered
journeys to be unearthed.

How can we undo the hurt that has been done?
How can we be found when all is lost and dark?
How can we learn to rise and dance again?

But rising from the ashes, powerful phoenix: a
mythical and sacred bird
Sacred bird, transcending dreams of hope and
transcending our desires.
Our desires, magical healer; harbinger of
restored faith and resilient courage.

Guardian angel, we learn like you: we rise again
and are reborn too.

Beautiful Monster

As I stand at the edge of the shore, it feels
misleadingly sure
To see the sand framed by the infinity of the sea.
I stare until my eyes can see no more just
The vague meeting of sky blue with sea green.

To me, the tranquil horizon appears like an azure
smirk, of false
Glittering charm. Maybe the beauty is masking
the terrifying turbulence below.
But above, the calm surface convincingly
conceals the rough rip tide beneath
And with a cloaked-smile, the sea's surface,
cunningly pulls and tugs on my soul.

I, with trepidation, leave the shore's edge to
wade into the cold
Unknown. Maybe the unpredictable monster is
lurking threateningly bold beneath.
Deep down, resting, with its emerald eyes,
cavernous mouth; sharp, coral teeth
And waiting patiently to swallow its bait, to
capture and imprison my grief.

With a breast-stroke swim, my cold hands
cupping through waves
With legs like a frog in a pond full of weeds, I
feel the
Infinite monster near. Maybe it's remaining
deceptively volatile below
And its shadow is ominous and my swimming is
slow.

You are a beautiful monster, deceiving and
fragile as glass
You shine like a diamond and you are a
sea-sparkling star.
And whilst on the surface you are smooth and
serene
Below in the depths, I know your monster roar
screams.

As I turn to swim back, trying defiantly to get
closer to soft sands
My resilient strokes are striving to defy the
savage-wild waves.
And the tide is turning as I hear the beastly
storm-current calls.
But we must endure courage as the monster's
dark abyss is nothing to fear.

High School Teacher

Early morning, before the bell screams,
She breathes in the calm, she remembers lost
dreams.
Before the invasion ensues and the rebels defend
She pours a hot tea from her flask, her best
friend.

Desks are put into place, books are smartened
and straight
She rubs the board clean and rewrites the date,
Acknowledging, anniversary of Bard's birthday
and death,
She imagines rowdy beer-tavern and his final
last breath.

The bell loudly clangs, her daydream dispels –
She's back in the classroom; her heaven or hell.
But, today her witchcraft is magic, the spells that
she casts
Float through the classroom like tall ships with
full masts.

With enthusiasm and energy, she ignites the fire
That burns in her students, fuelling passion with
desire

With an omniscient eye, she knowingly shapes
their inescapable fate
Are they destined for greatness as their
unexplored futures await?

So let the bell clang, let heaven and hell chime
Chime heaven and hell, wisdom has transcended
in this precious time.
And like a sheep dog guiding its herd, with
principled morality and steel,
She boundlessly leads her flock with enduring
commitment and zeal.

The Church in the Hamlet

As I read the inscriptions carved into the stones
A final resting place, for faces now unknown.
Praises that memorialize the dead, above hollow
bones
Hollow bones, buried deep, at rest for eternity.
Solitary - alone.

Immortalise the human souls of the past
Families who once walked this fragile earth
Gracing their presence fleetingly, nothing made
to last
But their light keeps burning bright through
generations of birth.

No more will they love or experience pain
They are gone, life is short; it will come to us all
They have left their lives, some with fulfilment
and some dying in vain.
But their memories live on, voiced by sad
laments and poignant recall.

The church: a place of celebrations; pronouncing
husband and wife
Of sermons, hymns and prayers; the preaching
of heavenly woe.

A melancholy site to house oak coffins;
foreshadowing the transience of life.
To bury the dead, the definite funeral, to be hurt
and forced to let go.

Life is precious: a mighty concoction of
happiness and sorrow.
Is it better to die, than not to have lived at all?
Is it better to own today, than lose tomorrow?
Tomorrow, the harsh reality is decay, like an
autumn leaf, we all will fall.

Life is a juxtaposition of laughter and tears,
human souls feel
In their waking hours; grieving the deaths of
their departed most dear.
Little lives, short and slight: leaving only graves
for loved ones to kneel.
Little lives, once full of life but now remain
asleep, year after year after year.

Gap Year

Her husband left, so she thought she'd take a
risk.
She knew her family would regard her actions as
irresponsibly amiss.
After forty-five years of marriage, she threw
open her window wide,
Life is too short to vegetate, in one breath she
cried.

Getting old may come with its restrictions,
Its restrictions, tampered by frustrating
limitations:
Irritating pains in the hips, knees, toes - the list
goes on and grows and grows.
But at the age of seventy-three, she's too spritely
- she's not ready to decompose.

I'm going on a gap year, she boldly had to shout.
I'm going on a gap year, it's time for me to lock
up shop and bloody well go out.
I'm going on a gap year, I'm tired of mundane
boredom
So I'm going on a gap year for wild
abandonment and being random.

So she booked her flight to an exotic faraway
land
And like a teenager on a maiden voyage planned
She packed her rucksack and singly loudly
around her home
She felt as giddy as a child, allowed for the first
time to shop alone.

She twisted her thinning, grey hair up into a
loose bun,
She'd found her freedom - growing old surely
means being daring and having fun.
And she left. Just like that. No regrets or
hesitations.
Life is too short, as the old adage goes, for not
seeking wild vacations!

A year passed by, she'd reached seventy-four
Smugly soaking in the sun; not yet knocking on
heaven's door.
She'd found her home in Marrakech, a raid with
a clear, blue pool.
She raised her glass to her own success: life, for
her, a jewel.

Blank Canvas

Life is a battleground from the moment we are
born,
We are born surviving our first few hours,
unable to keep warm.
A baby cries vulnerable tears, being at the mercy
of its carer.
A bewildering world awaits the babe, for some it
could be fairer.

Some are born with silver spoons and some in
poverty.
Some are born in paths of gold and some where
people flee.
Naked babies begin the same but different
worlds they live,
And this governs what they do not have or what
they are free to give.

The world is a blank canvas, a palette for
endless art.
The story that is painted depends purely on our
part.
Our part could be pictures of privilege and
advantage; of wealth and liberty,

But our story could be downfall depicting
challenges and misery.

Some are born to hardship, amidst a perilous
storm
And may grow a steadfast spirit to fight against
their norm.
Adversity, is not their enemy but a protective,
resilient shield
Adversity is their armour, their fortitude, their
power that they wield.

Life is a battlefield, we fight until our last
breath.
We all are defeated in our final hours, we cannot
defy death.
But with death, we leave behind our painting -
our canvas marks our place
Our place in this world is now gone, but we
leave behind our painting
And depart without a trace.

Hubris

Take that self-important look off your
unimportant face
We know who you really are, you are a broken,
sad disgrace.
You were once a great soldier, respected, now
fallen from grace
All of your authority wiped off, gone, without a
trace.

You belittle your people with words of bitter,
hard contempt
You smash their aspiring victories with spiteful,
malicious intent.
You strive to make them fall, you will their dark
descent
When you feel insecure you don't step back, you
never, ever relent.

You may plough over my emotions like an army
tank at war
You do not pause to contemplate the flattening
of my soul.
You squash my reputation with your power and
control

But I will fight back one day, my blood you will
not ignore.

So take that self-important look off your
unimportant face.
You think you are victorious. You think that you
are ace.
Your hubris is your downfall; your crew is
jumping ship
And one deluded rat is left alone, all powerless
and weak.

Healing Powers

Let us venture into your woods where all is
timeless and free,
The ancient trees swish and sway, whispering
mysteriously.
The steadfast, old oak standing loyally tall for
hundreds of bygone years
It has its roots that heal, secure deep down
Anchoring away our fears.

Your nature's healing powers nurtures our
progress as we age,
We weave along your untrodden paths to restore
our every stage.
We appreciate your beauty, your undiscovered
glade
We understand how life is shaped by the
Choices we have made.

Let us venture across your meadow where gentle
cows graze and roam,
Where happy buttercups, as rich as gold, glow
warmly in their home.
Where beautiful flowers, our guardian angels,
their energy dispels our gloom

Our guiding lights radiating tranquillity and
strength, not
Fragile like us, at all.

So, let us venture into your woods embracing
your still warm air.
Can you hear our hearts and souls calling;
appreciate that we care?
Can you feel pity for our fleeting stay whilst you
in your wisdom grow?
And your rhythmic heart of nature will beat
through time and we will
Cease to know.

Final Full Stop

Life is like a novel, full of twists and turns.
Nights ending on cliff hangers, not knowing
what the sunrise will bring.
A life could be circular – it ends where it begins
Trapped in repetitive circles of misery and
despair.
Or an unpredictable mid-life fantasy of
heightened climax and surprise.
A character's fate is hard to decipher, they might
suddenly die.
In every chapter we find moments of joy and
sorrow
The tapestry of mankind woven through plot,
every novel ending with a full stop.
We meet in life characters that are true and bad,
false and kind
A rich depiction of the wealth and range of the
diversity of human kind.
But reaching the final chapter, with only a few
lines left,
Has your life been rich and full or mainly
regretful discontent?
Life, what a story, what an adventurous read – a
book you can't put down.
Embrace and enjoy each chapter, until you reach
that final full stop.

How

How can we love our children more when are
hearts are bursting at the seams?
We have steadfast ribs that cage our hearts like
iron railings protect a home.
But ribs can break, snapping our certainty, like a
burglar's chrome bar shatters
A wrought iron lock. But like a seamstress with
a thread, confidence can be repaired.

How can we not miss our children when
memories become distant ghosts?
Their laughter's echo, fading haunts, in the silent
chambers of our souls.
Chilling and cold like an empty funeral parlour
after the mourners have gone
We grieve for their youth. Metamorphosis steals
our child - ages and transforms.

How can we not fret and flutter when an
airborne child takes flight?
Like a novice pilot in a violent storm, we fear
them crash landing in their prime.
But we grow strong. Like a sentry on duty, we
keenly watch them navigate to

Independence, and in the line of duty, we catch them when they fall.

Shame

Like a spark, his temper flared and he was angry
– shouting
Cruel words of accusation and blame, his nerve
holding
Fixing his eyes at the blurred vision in front of
him, determined
To have his say, not realising the power of his
intent as he
Hit the enemy line, his words firing painfully at
her as
A third degree burn agonises the skin;
The hatred in his scathing eyes, regretting every
moment of
Her being his wife. Embarrassed to see her
standing there
In front of his friend. The uninvited guest, gate
crashing
The inner sanctuary of their home -

Exposed, naked – ambushed: their private
emotions suddenly public
As though captured on film and once shot,
unable to be edited or erased.
They had been overheard, seen, witnessed – and
they felt ashamed.
As she fled from the room like a bird startled by
a fox

She nervously hid, on edge in her own home, listening to
Their superficial light-hearted chat as though
She had disappeared into dust off the face of the earth.
And no more words were said or touched on again,
After his arrival – his intrusion that interrupted
An unfinished row.

Later, he went back to tending to his plants, with his bare hands
Gently dead-heading their buds like the most loving
Romantic that ever graced upon this world.
The wilted flower drooped whilst he remained absorbed, oblivious
To her suppressed cries. She felt like an unwanted weed wastefully surviving
In his neat and tidy garden. He silenced her.
And he knew that it hurt, so he twisted the knife. She is his wife,
He is in charge and today he manipulates
And makes things right again when it suits him –
Like a king on a throne in front of his dignities.
Today, she is incarcerated in a marriage prison - a
Shackled, debilitating cell.

Looking Back

There was something about the way that you looked at me that day.
That day you held a look so cold and terrifying it has stuck with me until now.
Even though thirty years have passed, I still remember that cold, hateful glance.
That hateful glance, frozen into place like a solid ice cap on the Arctic Sea on a sub-zero winter's night.

Your look was frozen. I was frozen. Even the sun was frozen.

Looking back, I think you might have chucked me under the nearest bus as we argued along the high street, that day.
Looking back, I think you might have afterwards fled down the high street blaming your crime on the old lady in front of you, that day.
That day, an old lady innocently dragging her shopping trolley along the pavement, trying to avoid the cracks in the pavement.
Once, she did get hit by a speeding car and broke her hip.
She stayed in hospital for five weeks -

The speeding car flung her up into the air and
she had only gone out for five minutes to buy a
loaf of bread.

And now, I don't know why your face is in my
mind today.
I don't know why I remember that particular
look today.
Maybe it's because today I still love you.
Maybe it's because today I miss our stupid,
futile rows.

Our stupid futile rows that dissipate into
insignificance because you are gone.

And I miss you.

Mr Brown

You are brown:
Your eyes, your hair, your shoes, your tweed
jackets
And brown wool jumpers and corduroy trousers
–

The day I saw you I called you Mr Brown –
Mr Brown, the respected school teacher with
Brown leather patches on his elbow sleeves
Of his tweed jacket.
Mr Brown, serious, drab Mr Brown.

But you were never a teacher.
You would have liked to have been a train driver
–

You would always walk along the platform to
the very end
When waiting for the train. Didn't matter if it
was raining.
You had your brown jacket to keep you warm
and anyway
You didn't mind the rain like I did.
I kept shelter like a rabbit in the middle of an
exposed field
Jumping gleefully into its little hole.

And I liked travelling with you, Mr Brown – it
felt romantic and old fashioned
A bit like you.

Once I saw you as a little boy carrying a very
large brown briefcase
This oversized brown briefcase that suited your
style.
You didn't notice me as I watched you wait for
your mother
For a lift home in her little red car.
I was a dancing bright-eyed eight year old – you
a mature man of eleven.
There I stood, watching Mr Brown with his
over-sized briefcase squeeze into
His mother's car. Sitting awkwardly in the front
seat, the brown briefcase was bigger than Mr
Brown's head.
Who would have thought that I was watching
my future husband get into that car, on that
brown autumn 1978 dreary afternoon?
But brown autumn soon changes to yellow
summer.

And it was in that yellow summer of 1993 that
Mr Brown wore a dashing, cream
Wedding suit and in the brilliance of our lives
We became Mr and Mrs Kaleidoscope of Colour

With our patterns frequently changing, over the years, shifting with every turn.

Thank you - my Mr Brown with your over-sized brown briefcase
Thank you my colourful brown rainbow of joy.

Altered Destinies

I wonder what my life would be if I had missed
that train, that day.
That day, I wonder what your life would be if
you had not sat next to me.
I wonder how a minute could have changed the
direct focus of our lives
And I wonder how altered our destinies would
be if we, had not met, by chance.

I wonder if you would have been happy in a
different life -
With different house, different wife and a
handful of different kids.
I wonder if you would have the job that you
have now or doing something else.
And I wonder if your something else would be
better than your something now.

I wonder where I would be calling home and if
fate had burdened me
Or would, I wonder, be graced by fate and the
finality of its choices.
But in the end, we caught that train and bound
by space and time
Fate has destined us to live shared lives, to be as
one, together.

Trust

I need you not to crack
When I walk across your lake of ice.
I need you not to break
When I drop you, china vase.

I need you not to burst
When I fill you with my air, balloon.
I need you not to snap
When I tighten your strings, guitar.

I need you not to let me down,
When I'm trusting you with my faith.
I need your trust, my life
Is in your hands.

But you do freeze my hope
Like I've fallen into a frozen lake.
And you do smash my dreams
Like I'm a china vase shattering into a million
pieces.
And do burst my goals
Like I'm a balloon suddenly going bang.
And you do snap my confidence
Like I'm a guitar string being pulled too tight.

But I won't be putty in your hands.

As I need you not.

I have my love who won't betray
And stays steady and strong.
My love is my solace –
Faithful and loyal to the end.

We are as one.

We have trust.

Milton Keynes UK
Ingram Content Group UK Ltd.
UKHW042120210624
444555UK00015B/816